Identifying the Broken Pieces

How Can You Fix What You Cannot Identify?

Angela Lee-Easter
Pictures by Angela Lee-Easter

© 2008 by Angela Lee-Easter

Published by Your Destiny Productions
Roanoke Rapids, NC 27870
www.YourDestinyProductions

Printed in the United States of America

All rights reserved. No part of this publication may be reproduced, stored in a retrieval system, or transmitted in any form or by any means- for example, electronic, photocopy, recording—without the prior written permission of the publisher. The only exception is brief quotations in printed reviews.

Lee-Easter.
      Identifying the Broken Pieces: How can you fix what you cannot Identify?

Unless otherwise noted, all biblical passages referenced are from The Holy Bible, Authorized King James Version ®. *The New King James Bible: New Testament and Psalms,* (Thomas Nelson, Inc, 1994)

https://www.facebook.com/identifyingthebrokenpieces/
angela.lee.easter@gmail.com
http://angelaleemoody.wixsite.com/destinyproductions
yourdestinyproductions.com@gmail.com

Dedications

I dedicate this book to my Lord and Savior, first and foremost. I dedicate this written expression of God's promises to make one whole to my loving and supportive husband, Rodney Easter, who has demonstrated the love of Christ in all obedience, loving his wife as Christ has commanded; to Shafia, Joydan, and Jeremiah, my gifts of joy, my children; to my little ones Nevaeh and Dewayne, my grandchildren; to my mother, Joyce, who has continued to make a difference in my life; to Mother Vanessa, the greatest mother-in-law on this side of heaven, who blesses me with her wisdom and love; to my sisters and brothers, who were destined to be in my life; and to my spiritual midwife, Stephlyn Turner, who has always embraced her duties with joy no matter the heaviness. I thank God for you all. You are in my heart.

Angie

Acknowledgments

First and always, I would like to acknowledge my Lord and Savior Jesus Christ, who inspired the words of this book. To Him be all praise, glory, and honor. Amen.

Secondly, I would like to say thank you to those of you who played an integral role in the fulfilling of my destiny and the writing of this book: Rodney Easter, Joydan, Jeremiah, Shafia, Stephlyn, Vanessa and Samuel Rivers, Michelle and David, Arthur Jarrett and the Heavenly Voices, the Roanoke Valley Early College staff and students—my family away from home—and my ECOD family. I could go on and on, acknowledging every individual who blessed, inspired, and prayed for me, but that would be another book. Nonetheless, I am truly thankful for each and every person whom God has weaved into my destiny. You are loved and appreciated.

Contents

Identifying the Broken Pieces   1
The Breakers   5
My Broken Pieces   6
Now What?   10
It Was Mine   11
Hard to Love with a Broken Heart   12
Counting Your Losses As Gains   13
The Bigger Picture   15
To Rebuild, You Need a Blueprint   16
The Parts of the Human Heart and Its Functions   18
The Parts of the Spiritual Heart and Its Functions   19
Broken Pieces   21
You've Been Set Up 22
Part of Me   24
God Wants to Talk   25
The Other One Man (Man/Woman) 26
Upset the Environment   29
Spiritual Immunity   31
Close the Door   33
Holy Hit Man   35
Strength Is Found in Endurance   37
My Captivity   38
Starting Over   39
Free to Love 40
The Value of a Man with a Full Inheritance   43
My Superman   44
My King   46
A Holy Life, with a Holy Wife/A Holy Stand with a Holy Man   47
Is It Real?   49
Removing the Magnet 51
Where Is Your Hope?   52
Let Go   53
Release It   55
It Still Hurts   56
Especially Yours   57
Easy to Love You   58
Your Wait Is Ordained; It Is Not in Vain   59

It Is Almost Over   60
My Lord   61
Reality Check   63
Learning to Forgive   65
You Can Make Mistakes; Don't Let Mistakes Make You   66
All Good and Perfect Gifts Come from God   67
Now Take His Head   69
My Song in the Night   70
Breathe on Me   71
He Is in the Midst   72
My Refuge   73
Your Wounds Are Still Tender   74
You Were in Him   75
In the Hands of God   76
Don't Retaliate; Let God Fight   78
Battle Scars   80
Deal with It Now   81
Something Better Is Coming   82
Made for Me   83
Where Is the Line Located?   84
What Is the Next Step?   85
God Is Good   86
Do You Remember?   87
Who Is This Man?   88
Know Your Judas   89
Take the City   91
Not Everything Will Be a Struggle   92

Identifying the Broken Pieces

When your heart has been broken and you have encountered many hurts, healing is required. It seems that those hurts have damaged you to the point of no return, and with each pounding of the heart, life is released. You are wounded, you are bleeding, and you are dying. However, not all is lost. There is a way to mend the wounds, there is a way to experience healing, and there is hope.

You are dealing with things that may be a result of the past or present. Nevertheless, each time your heart is broken and each time a blow is inflicted, it devastates you spiritually, emotionally, physically, and mentally. You find yourself curled up in a fetal position, wondering why there is so much pain.

You must realize that your heart has been dismembered. It is in what are called pieces because they are separated and broken from each other, but when they are placed together in their original state, they regain their former identity as a whole. Once its former state has been recovered, it can be identified as your heart and you as its true owner, as intended by the Lord.

This dissection was caused by various situations in your life. You must keep in mind that pieces are caused—they are not created. The who, the what, and the why are responsible for the breaks. It may have been a relationship, a family member, a job, or even a child. There are many reasons pieces are separated from the wholeness of one's heart. Each detached piece is a result of a specific situation you are in or will encounter; detachment will continue until identification and recovery have taken place.

Every piece that has been disconnected from the wholeness of the heart has a new owner. Many times, the new owner did not acquire the piece as a result of theft or force; rather, the piece was freely given. You released your heart, trusting that it would be handled with care. Nonetheless, if this condition remains, the dismantled pieces will be the property of what or who caused its condition. You will no longer have any control over what was once yours.

Before you can begin to heal the hurts and gather the pieces of your life, you will have to acknowledge that there are breaks. You will also have to recognize that you have changed because of the removal of what you needed to be whole. To begin the healing process, you must first identify the broken pieces. To identify the broken pieces, you must label them and identify their new owners. These steps are imperative to regaining ownership.

How many pieces were split off because of your life experiences? Whether there are two or fifty of them, you must go to God for instructions about how to put the pieces back together. He will direct you in locating and identifying each piece. Once you have realized who and what has control of the pieces, you can recognize and recover them.

You see, each piece has a new owner. If it is still broken, then it belongs to the breaker. Once you have labeled the piece and evaluated the effects its brokenness has had on your life, then and only then can the mending begin.

What did it prevent you from accomplishing? What lessons did you miss because of the missing pieces? Once you have answered these questions, you can move to the next stage of recovery. When you have realized that others are involved in your condition, you can initiate the healing. It is impossible to fix what you cannot identify. It is your job to position yourself for healing. The decision to regain control will provide an opportunity for you to progress to the next level of spiritual maturity.

As you begin to see each piece and its transformation, you will start to release some hurts, some brokenness, and many disappointments. You will have many answers to why your life has been on a never-ending downward spiral. Now there is a clear view of why you have become distant, depressed, suicidal, and unforgiving. It is because the pieces missing contained brotherly love, joy, life, and forgiveness. Regaining the pieces will require you to follow God's leading as He guides you through each stage of connecting your broken pieces.

When you are dealing with broken pieces, you are also dealing with displacement. As a consequence, you are responsible for not only connecting the pieces but also placing them in the correct position. You may ask why God can't handle this job. Simply put, He did not cause the condition. He has given you the power and ability to do what is necessary to accomplish the task.

There are places, positions, and levels you will never reach as long as these conditions exist. You cannot walk in the fulfillment of your destiny and trust in God for the outcome when your heart is in pieces. It will only cause unnecessary disappointments. To move on to the next levels of God's instructive living, you must be made whole.

You have been walking in your call, and up to this point there were no major interruptions or capturing moments. However, at the place you are about to go—where your feet will tread and where your spiritual vision will perceive destiny—it will be necessary to identify each piece and possess it. Each piece holds what you need to successfully carry out the mission to which God appointed you.

The Breakers

If a piece exists, there must be a break. Therefore, there must be breakers. These breakers caused the pieces' existing conditions. They created your new identity and the new identity of the place from which the piece was removed. However, identifying and labeling the pieces will ensure healing, mending, and possession. Breakers may come in many forms. They will appear to be genuine, and at times they will be.

Consequently, your connection with the breaker will result only in a disconnection, as the breaker possesses a piece of your heart.

My Broken Pieces
We All Have Them, but How Are They Identified and Labeled?

REL

The removal of this piece resulted in aggression, resentment, and issues with self-esteem. It was a piece with the power to create anger in the early stages of life, once removed. The empty space stimulated certain emotions toward people and affected the normal child development process. It also produced a spirit of domination when there should have been submission.

RING

This piece not only suffered separation, but its breaker took something that could never be replaced. Although its taking was consensual, the breaker robbed as a thief disguised as a friend. In turn, this created a longing to find what was taken—but only to discover guilt in the search.

KEM

This breaker had the ability to embrace for only a season, leaving an attachment that requires a lifetime commitment. This piece was taken with no intention of ever being returned. As a result, there is anger, bitterness, stolen youth, and unwanted responsibility. Now that it is no longer connected to the greater piece, it leaves the heart in solitude and fragmented.

RUN

This piece is a promise piece. It identifies the character of the breaker. Although many promises are made, they are never kept and never can be. My tradeoff for this interaction was distrust. Initially the breaker would provide emotional support and an appearance of friendship to gain confidence; nevertheless, it was short lived, as the piece was torn away. The resulting void did not remain, but greater disappointment took its place.

RAN

This was the greatest piece taken, although size does not matter to the breaker. The greater the piece taken, the greater the condition it creates. This breaker was a piece of work; it had the ability to cause spiritual draining, resulting in the natural person's dependencies growing stronger. The breaker struggles with self-esteem and self-assurance, so therefore it is dependent. This dependency caused a rise in my self-esteem and confidence. However, I had now become a carrier, and my personality was altered. This breaker became so dependent that it resulted in exhaustion from the responsibilities of carrying, motivating, and controlling. The removal of this piece was long term, so the damage it caused was deep.

ROD

This was a breaker with good intentions, but it did not have what it takes to follow through. This breaker was a hope builder. In the end, there was never a foundation to build upon, only empty promises.

Everything about the removal of this piece ended in failure. This breaker had a fear of moving forward because of the unknown. For that reason, this breaker could only begin to run but could never finish the race.

CRUD

The thing about this breaker is that a lack of awareness caused it to break unintentionally. The breaker suffered from fear and anxiety. These are also the conditions left in place of the broken piece. Because of the fear that torments this breaker, it cannot move on. The unfortunate thing about the relationship was that the breaker wanted a companion in stagnation. Because the breaker hid behind things such as the word of God and works, never allowing development to become productive and mature, stagnation was always imminent.

Such breakers are trapped in the misconception that strengths are found in isolation, simply staying in the same position, refusing to move, and preventing others from getting close; this creates a wall of safety for them. The fear of change and newness generated anxiety for the breaker. Easily sidetracked by life's situations, the breaker became overwhelmed, and the broken piece was dragged down a road of afflictions.

JM3

Initially, this did not appear to be a breaker. This breaker had the ability to break as a result of personally suffering from many broken pieces. Broken people break others. It may not always be intentional, but it is evitable. This breaker carried pains and failures of the past and the present.

The piece that was taken left a space to be filled with the conditions of the breaker. These are the same results with each piece taken. The pains and failures of this breaker were disguised, but as the piece was pulled away from the ever-diminishing greater piece, the breaker's true identity was exposed.

As it tore away, leaving wounds, scars, and exposed flesh, I knew more about what had caused my emptiness. The breaker did not hide weaknesses; there was an unspoken desire to be healed from the ever-present afflictions suffered.

For this very reason, wholeness is necessary before unifying or attaching in any form. In addition, your condition is not the only concern; whom or what you attach to must be whole as well. If an attempt is made without healing, you will be left with many dislocated and broken pieces.

Mason

I refuse to believe that this could ever be a breaker. I invested what was left of the piece and gave it freely. Because of my actions, the piece was shattered and discarded as if it had no meaning or worth. I thought I was making the right choice, but I soon realized that this breaker was fully aware of the intentions of breaking. I was left with self-loathing, low self-esteem, and brokenness, and death seemed like a quiet escape.

ME

The last breaker took the final piece that controlled more than will ever be known. This breaker could have prevented any detachment. This breaker could have rested in the Master's arms, but instead sought what appear to be the answers. Instead, she broke the final piece of herself, causing more damage to an unrecognizable heart

Now What?

It is a sad situation to have pieces of your heart removed by people, places, or circumstances. The sad truth remains that the conditions of the breakers will likely become your conditions. The space that is left must be filled, and the nearest filler is what you are exposed to at the time. This is not to say that you are extremely weak or very easily taken. In fact, your existing condition solicited such breakers, asking them to come into your life. This is the reason why it is absolutely imperative that you give your heart to the Lord, no matter the condition.

Now that you have realized what is involved with unidentified pieces and the breakers that cause them, you can recognize and label them. You are now able to locate, regain, and rename the pieces. When you are again in ownership, you will place the identity that should have been there in the beginning, which is My Lord. God should have ownership of your heart. That will prevent it from falling unexpectedly into the hands of the breakers.

It will also allow the one who has been ordained by God to hold your heart as precious. Now that God has possession, the only way your heart can be released is by seeking the face of God. You chose the breakers and allowed the damage, whether it was known or unknown, but now you have the power to keep your heart in reserve for the person God has predestined. You are hidden in Him, never to be broken again.

It Was Mine

I was born with it. It belonged to me,
But I trusted too many and now I am left empty.

How can I regain what once was mine?
Can I just ask and have it returned in time?

How could this happen? I am a child of God.
I thought His love would guard me and my heart.

But it was by my free will it was taken away.
To regain it, I must stay before God and pray.

Although I am at fault all alone,
My heavenly Father will never leave me on my own.

He will teach me what must be done.
Then it will return to where it belongs

Only to give it away once again
To the one that is my beginning and my end.

To you, O God, do I give my heart,
To be secure and never again torn apart.

Hard to Love with a Broken Heart

When you suffer breaks, it will be very difficult to love. What you have encountered with the breakers and the pieces has the power to hinder loving, trust, caring, or even committing. It is God's will that we love one another. This is how the world will identify that we are the sons of God.

A broken heart is the kind of damage that can change your character, condition, and position. It has a stronghold. It is able to keep you under burdens and bound to the things God has set you free from. The effects of such an emotional blow can cause devastation.

You may have been a very caring person who was willing to help people the best way you could, but because of your broken heart, your character has changed. You are no longer caring or willing to lend yourself out because you have decided people have an alternative motive. Now you have become the skeptic. You are not free to love.

The bondage of your brokenness has caused you to be captive to various weaknesses. Things you would not do in the past you have begun to compromise on. You have become enslaved to the results of a broken heart. You are held in captivity by the breakers. How could you love in such a condition?

Counting Your Losses As Gains

Because of the things you have suffered, what has been lost? What has fallen away because of the struggle to mend or reattach broken pieces? Look at the losses. Look at the friendships, relationships, jobs, or even life experiences that you have avoided because of these situations. These situations are the events associated with each piece. So now, count your losses.

As you evaluate the losses, you will begin to appreciate what has happened. You look at some friendships and realize that if those friendships had been allowed to continue, it would have added to the dilemma. The friendship would have damaged your reputation. It would have stolen what you have worked so hard to accomplish. Now then, was it really a loss?

That relationship you worked so hard to make work has fallen completely apart. You prayed to God for its success, hoping it would result in a lifetime partner, but it ended. As you examine the relationship, as you stand back and look at what you really had, you see it all too clearly. It was dominating, possessive, and demeaning. Was it really a loss?

You really wanted that job. You prepared yourself mentally, physically, and spiritually, hoping you would get the call. When you never got the confirmation call, you were very disappointed and went to the Lord with an attitude. "Lord, why didn't you make it happen for me?" You have had some time to really think about it. Now you realize that this job would have kept you from church, family, and friends. The pay was good, but the price you would have paid would have cost you your life, joy, and peace. Ask yourself, Was this really a loss?

Each thing that you have considered a loss has placed you in a position to prosper, excel, increase, and find peace. Your so-called loss has placed you in a gaining position. You have more because of what you were denied. Have you not acknowledged yet that God will move anything and everything out of your way to secure success?

When things do not happen your way, count it all joy: He just enlarged your territory. Now you have space to accommodate a greater blessing.

The Bigger Picture

You have fixed your eyes on a particular thing, assuming it is the thing you need. This thing appears to be able to solve your present problem. However, this minuscule, small thinking will hinder the move of God in your life. Instead of focusing on a particular element in a masterpiece, look at the entire creation. What you fail to realize is that each part works together to express a grand design. If you leave out the simplest piece, you will end up with an incomplete expression.

The bigger picture represents the many things you will encounter in your life. For instance, as you begin to put the pieces back together, you will not only experience healing, which is only a small part of a big picture but also regain identity. You will also be able to let people into your heart, because of its wholeness. You will be able to recognize the breaker and guard your heart with all diligence.

As a result of the past and present, and even God's future plans, you have become a greater person. You are His Masterpiece. You are more than a piece or a part; you are an original, and as you grow and develop in the Master's hand, you will begin to realize the need for everything you have been exposed to. You will indeed appreciate and find joy in being created and designed by a hand so skillful, so gentle, and so masterful. You are the bigger picture, the very expression of God's love.

To Rebuild, You Need a Blueprint

You have regained the pieces and acknowledged their conditions and positions. What do you do next? Well, your next step is to assemble them, remembering they are out of place. Where do they go? This is the time when you must seek the Father for instruction. Each piece has a specific position; they work together to keep the flow of necessary emotion, affections, desires, compassion, and even forgiveness continuous.

Making this a little simpler, let's look at the natural man's heart and its makeup. You will observe that each part is positioned to keep the flow of blood accessible to each part of the body. This awesome dance ensures life continuance. Likewise, the positions of the spiritual heart are fashioned to keep love flowing within and without.

The Parts of the Human Heart

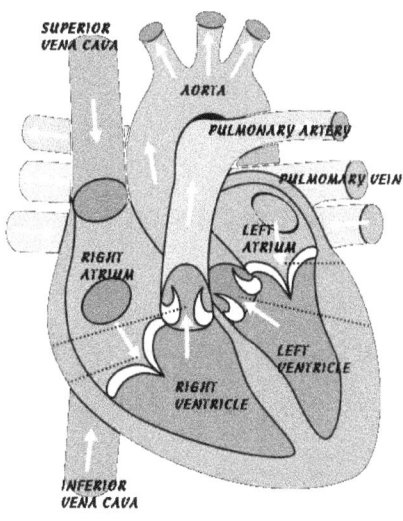

The Parts of the Spiritual Heart

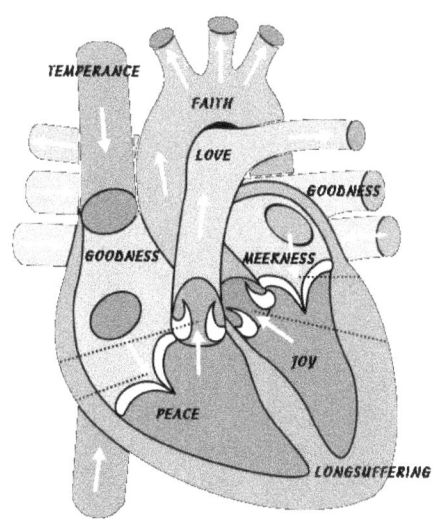

The Parts of the Human Heart
and Its Functions

- Superior Vena Cava—conveys blood from the head, chest, and upper extremities
- Aorta—conveys blood from the left ventricle of the heart to all body parts except lungs
- Pulmonary Vein—a vein that carries oxygenated blood from the lungs to the left atrium of the heart
- Right Atrium—the upper chamber of the heart that receives blood from the vena cavae and coronary sinus
- Left Atrium—the chamber on the left side of the heart that receives arterial blood from the left atrium and pumps into the aorta
- Mitral Valve—regulates blood between the left atrium and left ventricle
- Pulmonary Valve—an artery that carries venous blood from the right ventricle of the heart to the lungs
- Aortic Valve—guards the passage of blood to prevent its backward flow
- Left Ventricle—receives arterial blood from left atrium and contracts, forcing it into the aorta
- Right Ventricle—receives venous blood from right atrium and forces it into the pulmonary artery
- Tricuspid Valve—three segmented valves that keep blood in the right ventricle from flowing back into the right atrium
- Interior Vena Cava—conveys blood from all parts below the diaphragm

The Parts of the Spiritual Heart
and Its Functions

Love—Doesn't delight in evil but rejoices in the truth. "Rejoiceth not in iniquity, but rejoiceth in the truth" (1 Corinthians 12:6 KJV).

Joy—The Joy of the Lord is your strength. "Then he said unto them, Go your way, eat the fat, and drink the sweet, and send portions unto them for whom nothing is prepared: for this day is holy unto our Lord: neither be ye sorry; for the joy of the Lord is your strength" (Nehemiah 8:10 KJV).

Peace—Therefore, since we have been justified by faith, we have peace with God through our Lord Jesus Christ. "Therefore being justified by faith, we have peace with God through our Lord Jesus Christ" (Roman 5:1 KJV).

Longsuffering—Forbearing on another in love. "With all lowliness and meekness, with longsuffering, forbearing one another in love" (Ephesians 4:2 KJV).

Gentleness—Kindness. "By the word of truth, by the power of God, by the armor of righteousness on the right hand and on the left" (2 Corinthians 6:7 KJV).

Goodness—"Wherefore also we pray always for you, that our God would count you worthy of this calling, and fulfill all the good pleasure of his goodness, and the work of faith with power" (2 Thessalonians 1:11 KJV).

Faith—"That he would grant you, according to the riches of his glory, to be strengthened with might by his Spirit in the inner man; That Christ may dwell in your hearts by faith; that ye, being rooted and grounded in love" (Ephesians 3:16–17 KJV).

Meekness—"With all lowliness and meekness, with longsuffering, forbearing one another in love" (Ephesians 4:2 KJV).

Temperance—"And beside this, giving all diligence, add to your faith virtue; and to virtue knowledge; And to knowledge temperance; and to temperance patience; and to patience godliness; And to godliness brotherly kindness; and to brotherly kindness charity" (2 Peter 1:5–7 KJV).

Unless otherwise noted, all scripture quotations in this publication are from [The New King James Bible, New Testament and Psalms. Thomas Nelson, Inc, 1994].

Broken Pieces

It was whole when it all begin,
But each time, a piece was taken away in the end.

It was mine; yes, it belonged to me,
But the promises that were made left me oh, so empty.

It used to beat in perfect harmony,
But now it pounds out of rhythm, and its beats are killing me.

I opened it far too many times.
Now there are pieces misplaced and no longer mine

Lord, help me, my heart, to recover.
Then I will give it to you, my friend and my true lover.

You saw each time it was torn apart.
I did not listen. You warned me from the start.

There was no love left, not even a token,
Only the pieces scattered and a heart that was truly broken.

You've Been Set Up

As you glance behind, just before pressing forward, you will see heaping piles of wreckage. Now, look once more before you put it all behind you. Look at the heaps carefully. They were strategically planned. No, not Satan this time—it was your Father in heaven! Oh yeah, He knew exactly what it was going to take to get you to move forward. It worked, didn't it?

You are where you should be. If it were not for the pieces of wreckage, you would have never realized your value, your importance, your predestined position. Now, let's reminisce. Remember when you met that person and he or she wreaked havoc in your life? Nevertheless, as years passed and you began walking in your preordained call, you were faced with some of the same things you experienced with that person.

You easily overcame those attacks because you had defeated them in the past. You embraced the truth that allowed you to see the setup. Your life was designed for you to meet certain people, work on certain jobs, and encounter certain situations. This is the reason associations are to be carefully evaluated because they can produce meaningful life connections. Associations are not just a happenstance; they are sometimes created so that you will gain favor. This favor will open doors and create avenues of success.

Open your eyes. God is 100 percent involved with your triumphant victories. You thought you were figuring it all out. It is definitely not you; it is the invisible hand of God. Although the breakers caused some serious displacements, they too are an important part of your setup. You will not experience anything that you cannot overcome a second time. If you took advantage of the opportunity the first time the situation was presented, you should be more aware. Your life is no surprise to God. He knows the end from the beginning.

He sees you in your triumphant moments and your moments of failure. They will teach you if you allow them. The way was prepared for you a long time ago. Your parents were chosen to conceive such precious offspring. You are not a mistake! You were a planned pregnancy. Now the time has come to gather the pieces, put them in their proper places, and take advantage of this setup.

Part of Me

She is my woman, lost in God's embrace,
A priceless treasure to be found in only one place.

At the feet of Jesus is where she hides,
Finding refuge in God's word is where she abides.

She is my woman like none I have ever seen.
I am her kingly lover, and she is my godly queen.

She is my woman, a gift to behold.
God designed her just for me and then broke the mold.

She is my woman, a treasure I have found.
She is the only woman in my kingdom.
She holds my scepter and my crown.

She is my woman; she is bone of my body.
I am found in her and she is found in me.

God Wants to Talk

Come now, and let us reason together, saith the Lord: though your sins be as scarlet, they shall be as white as snow; though they be red like crimson, they shall be as wool.
—Isaiah 1:18, KJV

Praise God, you have endured the trial, passed the tests, and stood against great temptation. Now you are faced with another test that is all too familiar. That test is the battle with yourself. You are finding out things about yourself that are really causing a struggle. You are looking in life's mirror and seeing warfare. What you must focus on is the promises God has made to you. Your obedience to the will of God will alleviate many hardships.

Now, what do the struggles entail? Does this struggle involve you wanting to have your way? If that is the case, there is a simple solution. You must decide to give all to God at the beginning of this journey. It's time to hold fast to your commitment. The Lord is not far from you. He sees and knows all that you are going through. All the hurts and disappointments—He knows all the things you have suffered. Don't count God as slack concerning His promises; He is a sure help in time of struggle. If God is for you, who can stand against you?

You are your own worst enemy. How do you fight such an enemy? You must attack your enemy with the word of God. The word is a two-edged sword. Talk to the Lord about your struggles. Your answer is in worship and in praise. It is imperative that you not trust in the seen things. Look in the mirror and begin to speak to what I refer to as the other one man—not the other woman but the other one man. See, the other one man is in you, trying to get you to follow fleshly desires. This other one man wants to dominate. This other one man would have you silent and withdrawn, so that he can be in control and rule

The Other One Man

The one man has no specific gender, just a goal to take over. "The first man is of the earth, earthy: the second man is the Lord from heaven" (1 Corinthians KJV). This man has a mind of his own. He wants to dominate, control, and rule. He wants it to be all about him. This one man rejoices in recognition and events where the spotlight gives him exposure. With this being the case, it is wise to stay alert. The one man will sneak out when you least expect it. The obvious characteristic of this one man is that he intentionally overlooks and neglects the things of God.

The things of God are contrary to what this man wants to do. You will have to resist his persistent intention to take over your mind, body, and soul. In most cases, the breaks and the pieces are allowed to exist as a result of this man. This man never evaluates the situation: if it looks good, feels good, or fleshly gratification can be obtained, this man will allow the things that cause breaks. There is a constant fight with the spirit man, wanting to take over. It is in the flesh where you will find him. "For the flesh lusteth against the Spirit, and the Spirit against the flesh: and these are contrary the one to the other: so, that ye cannot do the things that ye would" (Galatians 5:17, KJV).

You have sought God that you would be strong in His power. The power of God is the only thing that will keep you from this man's domination. This one man is responsible for the times you have been fleshly and disobedient to the things you knew God told you to do. Fasting and praying are the only things that will cause this man to cease movement. You must also seek the face of God concerning everything you have questions about or things you are unsure about.

If you seek for success in the things of God, you must restrain the one man. You must not let him get an inch, because if he does, he will successfully take a mile. Of course, there will be days that you will walk in discontentment, doubt, and failures. You must pull up yourself by your bootstraps, regain your composure, and walk in authority. Unfortunately, the illusion of most Christians leans toward the belief that they are powerless when they are struggling.

This trick is his signature trick. He tries to persuade Christians to doubt their spiritual abilities, so that they will walk in the flesh. It may be said that if you are truly born again, there is no possibility of this happening. It may be true in most cases, but it depends on where your strengths are. It also depends on what you are encountering during your struggles. Whatever you are dealing with in the trials, temptations, or tribulations, look up and know there is a greater power that resides in you and that He will never leave you or forsake you.

Here are some of the things you will surely be presented with concerning the one man:

- Doubt—He wants you to doubt your God-given abilities.
- Fear—He wants you to be afraid to step out in your authority.
- Lust—He wants you to pursue the desires of the flesh and be distracted from the plan of God.
- Confusion—He wants you to be caught between two decisions.
- Lies—He lies to you constantly to persuade you that what he suggests is better for you.
- Betrayal—When this man deceives you, he will leave you to suffer, which will motivate you to seek God, for your redemption. Your seeking God causes the one man to flee for a season. You are in the presence of God, and this is the place where he will be exposed.

- Hopelessness—He wants you to feel hopeless, trusting in the here and now. He doesn't want you to hope in what's not seen. Your deliverance is not seen, but as you trust God, it will be manifested.

The important thing about this one man is that you must identify who he is and what his plans are. His identity is very obvious: he is you, the old you. The plans are to get back to that familiar place he once lived in before Christ, in your sin nature. This present place is uncomfortable and convicting to the one man. Recognize your position and your power. Keep him under the authority of the word of God, which is in you.

Upset the Environment

When you begin to communicate with the Lord, whether through praying, fasting, singing, or even worship, something special takes place. It is an amazing thing that you are doing. You may not even be aware of the magnitude of what is going on. When you touch God through your hunger for Him, it upsets the natural world. Nature cannot comprehend the things you are doing. You are speaking and worshipping the almighty, unseen God.

Just having faith in God and using it will cause a reaction in your surroundings. You may not see the manifestation of your faith instantly; however, continue to commune with the Lord. You may wonder at times, *What exactly am I looking for, and why am I believing in God?* In the spirit realm, God begins to deploy the angels to assist you in what you need, in what you ask, and in what you think. God has greatness in mind for you. Therefore, the more you speak in faith, the more you will cause change around you.

God is not like man. He is willing to listen as long as you have something to say. He loves your voice, the words you speak to Him of His kindness, His love, and His protection. How much more will He do for you when you praise Him for what He has already done? As you take time to speak to Him of His greatness, He places those words in His heart. This affair results in God moving and upsetting the atmosphere. The miracles in your life are results of your relationship and His abundant love for you.

A miracle is an event that is beyond natural comprehension. A miracle is the result of the natural, the normal, and the familiar being troubled. When you commune with God, it causes contractions in the environment, which in turn birth your miracles. So how about impregnating your environment with praise, which will produce the miracle you seek? What are you prepared to communicate with God that will perform the miraculous operation you need?

He stands as a great physician, specializing in the delicate procedure required to mend your heart. Just consider this for a moment: the operating physician is in love with you. Your heart is safe in His hands. As He operates, He thinks of the moments you've shared. He must do what is necessary to guarantee you will be in a position to change the environment with your love song to Him. Oh, He has already ordained and predestined your healing. It is the product of your praise.

Spiritual Immunity

Immunity (medical): a state of having sufficient biological defenses to avoid infection, disease,
; related to the functions of the immune system.

God is a spirit, and if He abides in you, then you have acquired spiritual immunity. What does this spiritual immunity advocates? With spiritual immunity, you have sufficient spiritual defenses supplied by God to avoid being invaded by unclean demon forces. Simply stated, unwanted spiritual invasions are unable to inhabit your body.

Now that spiritual immunity has been explained, let us look at the different kind of invaders: lying spirit, lustful spirit, suicide spirit, depressed spirit, violent spirit, hopeless spirit, doubtful spirit, and many more. These unclean spirits cannot invade you because the greater one lives in you. These sneaky demonic forces are defenseless because of Almighty God on the inside. Nevertheless, if they cannot directly invade, they will use the things around you to get the job done.

If they want to lower your self-esteem and get you to consider suicide, then they will send not a spirit of lying but an actual liar. This person will raise your hopes and get your trust and confidence. Suddenly this pretentious person will cause you to crash, because of abandonment. This is the work of the breaker. If this happens, then you must run to the healing hand of a redeeming Savior. The shortcomings of too many people is that they neglect to seek immediate healing from the true physician.

When you go to the Savior, He will dress you in the whole armor. The armor is equipped to prevent penetration of the attacks of your enemies. Notice, if you will, that the breastplate covers your heart. Satan knows your soft spots. If he can't get in, he will find a foothold. This is the reason why it is so important to stay in study, fasting, and prayer. Although he knows your weakness, you don't have to be vulnerable to his attacks. You are spiritually immune. The only spiritual forces that should have the ability to inhabit your body are the Father, the Son, and the Holy Spirit.

Close the Door

There are doors that should have been closed a long time ago. These doors are preventing you from moving on. There are levels to which you cannot ascend because of the things that stand in the doorway. You are still holding on to hope, when that expectation in the doorway is only an illusion. The door to this false hope has been closed; however, your side remains open. You are the only one holding on.

There is no closure for you, and you are waiting for that moment when you can be released from the entire situation. Your wait is in vain, because you have not acknowledged that you need to close your side. There are situations in your life that caused hurt and harm, and as long as the door is open, you will continue to suffer those hurts. You are grasping for hope where there is none. You must shut the door.

The door has to be closed in order to have peace about the thing that broke your heart. If the door continues to stay open, there is no possible way of mending the pieces together. At each door stands the breaker. The breaker that separated the pieces has control over it and its condition.

Consider the breakers at the door and why it is imperative that you close the door. If you suffer a broken heart because of a relationship, you will hold to the hope of mending that relationship as long as the door is open. Now, if the other person has closed the door and you are left to hunger or thirst for hopes of mending, you will keep the wound open. The door must be not only closed, but locked. It should never be opened again.

If you have lost a loved one to death or someone has turned their back on you and rejected you, such situations can create tragedy breakers. There is nothing you could have done to change the situation. Even so, there are doors opened in such matters that may lead to depression, low self-esteem, suicide, and retaliation. If you leave these doors open, you will not be the only one suffering. You will hurt others as well.

If you try to move on with the door open, you will lose a lot of experiences that could have catapulted you to another spiritual plateau. You are preventing spiritual maturity from taking place. The doors are hinged on your hopes. If you take these hopes away, the doors will be closed and locked. In doing so, you will be able to move on with your assignment, which is what God intended.

Holy Hit Man

The path on which you are walking was predestined. If you are in the will of God, then the path you are on was planned. You are close to the things God planned for you; you're at the peak of your blessings. Just keep in mind that the blessings are not for you alone. These blessings are designed for the kingdom. They are for the advancement of the kingdom. That is why God will not let you stray. He will not allow you to jeopardize His investment. He has spent many days, weeks, months, years, hours, minutes, and seconds developing you to carry this call. This is all because of the vow you made long ago. You vowed to go all the way, and He is holding you to that promise.

God will not let people into your life who could jeopardize the greatness in you. If you are positioned to bless the kingdom of God, He will begin to strategically put in order, ways of removing people from your life by any means necessary. A kingdom is involved. Therefore, prepare yourself to see drastic removals of potential distractions.

Brothers, you cannot allow your desire to have a woman to interfere with the work of the kingdom. My dear brothers, you have to stand still and work in the kingdom until God releases you to pursue a wife. Likewise, my sisters, we know too well that a relationship is what you have been seeking the Lord for. Sisters, God will position you to be found in the midst of your work for Him.

There are appointed times for you to be in relationships. Relationships are mentioned in the scriptures. They are considered to be somewhat a distraction when you are on a mission for the Lord. Surely, the scriptures are not suggesting that you should never be in a relationship. However, timing is everything. Relationships are not the only distraction; pursuing a career can also be a distraction.

Jobs can become walls that stand between your reasonable services to God. The <u>Holy Hit Man</u> is God, and if He needs to snuff someone or something out of your life to guarantee success in kingdom work, He will do just that.

If you insist that you want what you want, then you will stand responsible for the repercussions or damage caused by your insistence on having your way. That man or woman you desire to be with is not worth having the kingdom suffer lack. In due season, if you faint not, you shall reap a great harvest, including your natural desires. God is concerned about the whole man.

Strength Is Found in Endurance

He that endures until the end shall be saved. A characteristic of endurance is strength. Standing against the storm will surely build your physical strength and stamina. It takes a strong individual to stand against twenty-mile-per-hour winds in our natural world. Can you imagine the strength you need to push against such a storm with just human force? If you add in the rain or even hail, how will you endure? What makes a person want to endure such harsh conditions? It all depends on their desperation.

Where are you trying to arrive? Whom are you trying to reach? What are you trying to obtain? To stand against such a thing, there has to be a passion involved. You have to choose to press with intensity, and then your pressing against what seems impossible will build your strength.

The spiritual storms you face will have the same result. Your spiritual muscle will be built and you will be able to endure great trials in the future. Your spiritual muscle will keep you able to fight the good fight of faith. Each storm will make you stronger for the next one. Resistance is what is used as you push toward the mark of the higher calling during the storm. You will press, endure, and strain toward the goal before you gain the necessary abilities needed to overcome the things you will face.

Strength is found in endurance, Weakness is found in quitting.
You won't ever know the results unless you are there in the end.
—January 7, 2008

My Captivity

He holds me tightly—there's no thought of letting go.
His embrace is one I crave and long to know.

He found me in the midst of a storm,
Spoke to the winds and waves, and I suffered no harm.

I discovered pleasure in His captivity.
In it I am not alone, for it is He who has captured me.

He has captured my mind, my body, and my soul.
There are no pieces with Him; I am made completely whole.

I am overwhelmed with His presence night and day.
It is Him alone I worship and to Him alone I pray.

He is worthy of praise, honor, and all glory,
And in His arms I am reminded of our love story.

Starting Over

This is the point where you need to realize that you have to let all unnecessary things go. However, all those things may leave you naturally. You have for many years relied on things seen. You have relied on things that were not profitable to the kingdom. It is time to let those things go. Once you have released these unprofitable things, you will have to find a starting point.

This starting point will begin with God ruling your heart. He will master your life from this point on. This is what He wanted to do the entire time. Once you realize that the breakers are controlling you, you will desire change. Change will require renewal, restoration, and refreshment. The taking and the giving of your heart caused damage. Therefore, your heart, soul, mind, spirit, and body in most cases will need to be renewed.

There were moments you gave your essence away, with hopes of a return that would fill or complete you. Unfortunately, you were sadly mistaken. When you agree to render such a priceless possession, it is possible that you will never repossess it. If you are able to reclaim it, it will be with a fight, and yes, the violent takes by force. How badly do you want to be whole again?

You have to imagine your stuff back in your possession. Regain your merchandise. This is part of starting over. Once it is in your possession, there will be a process involved in you relearning yourself. You are in a new position. Having possession over the thing lost long ago will require you to adjust. Your new position with the possession will allow you to walk in completeness in your mission.

Free to Love

Freedom is a word that covers a lot of areas in a person's life:

- Liberty
- Lack of Restrictions
- Self-Determination
- Independence

Liberty

"For, brethren, ye have been called unto liberty; only use not liberty for an occasion to the flesh, but by love serves one another" (Galatians 5:13, KJV).

Liberty is a freedom that gives you control over what you choose to do. It puts you in a position where you have the authority to claim, obtain, and possess whatever is to be yours. It's your liberty.

Lack of Restriction

"Thus, saith the Lord to his anointed, to Cyrus, whose right-hand I have holden, to subdue nations before him; and I will loose the loins of kings, to open before him the two-leaved gates; and the gates shall not be shut" (Isaiah 45:1, MSG).

This is a position where you have no restrictions concerning freedom. You are complete in your ordained freedom. Nothing can hold you back from accomplishing your liberation.

Self-Determination

"All of you worthless people, get away from me! I am determined to obey the commands of my God" (Psalm 119:115, CEV).

This position you are determined to obtain because you have acknowledged it as yours. You are persuaded that your promise will be yours and that by any means necessary, you will be in a position to receive it. In so doing, your determination will bless the kingdom.

Independence

"But what I do, I will continue to do, [for I am determined to maintain this independence] in order to cut off the claim of those who would like [to find an occasion and incentive] to claim that in their boasted [mission] they work on the same terms that we do" (2 Corinthians 11:12, AB).

You are in control of your freedom, needing no one to persuade you of where you are positioned. You are now independent and able to handle each situation of the heart with liberty, needing no natural assistance. When you are aware of your liberties, your lack of restrictions, your self-determination, and your independence, you will also acknowledge your abilities and begin to operate in them. You are now free to love. You are no longer in the breakers' bondage.

You have taken what was rightfully yours. You are made whole. God has mended your heart, and you are free to love. Before, you were a slave to the breakers. Now that you have been set free, you are released from your taskmasters. These breakers not only had your pieces, but controlled areas of your life, because they substituted the piece with a condition.

You have to do what it takes, through the direction and instruction of the Holy Ghost. In doing so, you will be aware of how to obtain your freedom. If you want to love now, you can, because you are free from all restrictive elements. You are self-determined and will strive to enter through the straight gate. This gate was designed for those who are set free indeed.

The Value of a Man with a Full Inheritance

There are princes and then there are kings. There are many differences in their positions and titles. The differences between the two are sometimes obvious and sometimes not so obvious. Both are royalty. They both are required to respect kingdom authority. They both have the power to rule.

My Prince

All these things are true, but their royalty, authority, and the respect for their kingdoms are at different levels. A Prince is royalty, but he has no extreme requirements concerning the kingdom, no real life-changing expectations. His requirements are mostly dealing with preparation. A prince has to be prepared to rule, but has no kingly nor kingdom-changing authority.

Considering this information, a woman who is positioned to be in a relationship with such a man must realize many things. First of all, such a man walks in a degree of royalty, which is not a bad thing at all. Even though his being a prince makes him royal, this position prevents him from operating in full authority.

Then there is the matter of Kingdom respect. He does have respect from the kingdom, but it is a secondary respect. He is respected only because of the king and kingdom protocol. Lastly, concerning authority, a prince's authority is not that of running a kingdom, but authority over his own affairs.

My Superman

You are my superman,
A man who can wait on God and be still.

You are my superman,
Able to be honest with me and so real.

You are my superman,
Not afraid to say what's in your heart or how you feel.

You are my superman.
You said you love me; now our union is sealed.

You are my superman.
You look beyond the surface and can see within my heart.

You are my superman.
You are my man of steel and a man of God.

You are my superman.
You hold me in your arms like I am your queen.

You are my superman,
A strong man not afraid of anything.

You are my superman.

You did not remove a piece, but added to my heart.

You are my superman.
You are a man of integrity; you were honest from the start.

Believe me when I say your search is over now.
You have wanted to be loved, and I know how.

So, with my love, I freely give you my hand.
I am your superwoman, and you are my superman.

My King

A woman must allow a godly man to be the king of the relationship, because this man walks in a royal position with a full inheritance. The woman who seeks more than a prince, waits to be found by a true king. She knows and understands the value of a man who has received his full inheritance. A king is the absolute highest form of royalty, with all the accompanying expectations. He also has the utmost respect of his subjects. If they don't respect him, they would hardly make an outward display, for fear of sudden punishment. When it comes to authority, this man sets the mark.

This is the kind of man whom a woman prepared to be queen desires. Just as a man of God receives his inheritance (salvation) and is prepared to rule a kingdom, a woman receives her inheritance and has the power and authority to also rule a kingdom. These two—a spiritual king and queen—can unite and be a great value to the kingdom of God.

Now, a man who has not received his full inheritance but has potential to get it right has no business trying to rule or lead anything, because he doesn't have the kingdom backing him. The power that people possess when they have received their full inheritance enables them to set things in order. The power they possess was given by a greater power, which is God, the Father.

Mature Christians who have accepted their inheritance and walk in them in all obedience have no problem with following the instructions of God. Their royal positions and levels of authority will ensure a successful union. A man with an inheritance is of great value, as is the queen he marries.

A Holy Life, with a Holy Wife
A Holy Stand with a Holy Man

"Follow peace with all men, and holiness, without which no man shall see the Lord." (Hebrews 12:14 KJV)

"Let all your things be done with charity." (1 Corinthians 16:13 KJV)

The union between two holy people creates a life and a stand that is pleasing to God. A holy wife is a woman of integrity, and a holy man would be proud to have such a woman on his side in battle. She's strong and dependable. She desires to please God with her whole heart. In so doing her king will find complete pleasure in her.

She finds it delightful to be with such a man. He doesn't complete her; he is just an addition to all that God has already imparted and bestowed on her life. A holy man walks with the strength and abilities God has released on him for the building and edifying of the kingdom of God. He loves his wife as Christ loves the church. He is willing and ready to lay his life down to protect her.

He has no fear of death because of his eagerness to see the one who gave it all. He approaches each opposing situation with the whole armor of God on. Standing without wavering for God, family, and mission, he stands as a pillar. Those are just a few attributes of a holy man. To stand with such a man will be a great pleasure. His strength upholds a woman, and knowing that this is the result of loving a holy woman, he is strengthened even more.

Such a holy union will bless the kingdom of God. Their oneness will be observed and envied. Neither of them will be lost in each other, because although they are one, they possess their own identities. They have individual calls, ordained by God. As they minister to each other, they must also trust God to direct them in accomplishing their assignment. A holy man and a holy wife can cause a mighty move of God in their union.

Is It Real?

Make sure that God is leading you as you make steps toward your destiny. The devil will throw things before you to keep you bound. He has a plan for your life, and that plan is to destroy the plan that God predestined. Satan will send people, jobs, and other things to pull you away from that which is real.

You ask God if what you are doing is really what He has called you to do. It is Satan's job to delude you. He will delude you to a point where there is no room for recovery. God has a greater plan, and His plan must be played out for you to reach that place that will position you to bring glory to God and build the body of Christ.

He wants you to be about the mission. Because if you aren't, it will postpone the outcome. It won't stop the outcome. It only has the power to delay. If you recognize Satan's tricks, you can send him into confusion. You must confound the devil with your obedience to God. It doesn't matter how many tricks Satan sends; God has already placed everything before you to guarantee your success.

There are the breakers, the pieces, and the displacement—and don't forget the pain. All of these ingredients would cause most to assume this plan was successful. It was successful, but not for the reason claimed. It was a success because it caused you to seek God. It caused you to walk in obedience to the call, to identify each piece and put the pieces together. Now you are a person of strength and endurance. You are now what God intended you to be; He allowed the heartbreaking storm and the winds that tossed the broken pieces. Look back and observe that the pieces are no longer in the control of another.

What will you do now that you have regained the pieces? Will you give them to your Lord, or will you allow other breakers to come and repeat the whole thing? This is another trick of the enemy to steal your identity. He wants an instant replay, the lesson that you should have learned the first time will be presented again. The Lord would rather you learn the first time so you can move on with new knowledge.

In many instances, men and women go right back to the same situations over and over needlessly. These are situations from which the Lord has repeatedly delivered you. Why is this such a problem in the people of God? In simple terms, there is an attraction to a certain kind of man, woman, job, friends, or even food. It is something like a magnet: it pulls that thing in your direction and it pulls you in the direction where the thing abides.

Removing the Magnet

The things that attract you to hurts, pains, and brokenness must be removed. If they are removed, you will be able to avoid an attachment to people, places, and things that alter whom God desires you to become. You can adjust your attraction by seeking the face of God constantly. This will begin the process of eliminating the magnet and adjusting your attraction.

The difference between a Satan-placed magnet and an adjusted attraction is that a magnet will draw bad things to you. An adjusted attraction will attract only those things that cause you to be successful.

If your attraction is not adjusted through seeking God, you will accept what the magnet has drawn to you. If you seek God, you will be attracted and attached only to those things that add to your missions, your assignment, and your call. Don't think for a moment that Satan will sit back and not deploy an attack. He will send a delusion, a false reality, or a replica of the genuine thing. His tactics will be to no avail, because your seeking the Lord, will give you revelation concerning his plans. You must remain in a position to reject the breakers and their control over what God gave you to give Him.

Where Is Your Hope?

You have realized that the pieces were misplaced, dislocated, and unidentified. Now you begin, with the Spirit of God, to assemble, locate, and identify. You have work to do. Your hope is built on nothing less than Jesus's blood and righteousness. This is your assurance that the condition of your heart is about to experience a surgery from the *Chief Physician.*

The hope has been built on your knowledge of where your help comes from. You are walking in the fulfillment of your destiny, trusting God for the outcome. Now you are fully persuaded that the piece will be positioned to carry the name that is above every name. Although your confidence is secure, beware of the hope stealer. Satan wants you to leave your heart in a shambles, but in that condition, God cannot use you successfully. Satan can deceive you into thinking that you have lost. Grab hold of hope, faith, and love. That will cause you to experience the Lord moving greatly.

Hopelessness removes all possibility of success. Trust in the Lord and embrace the hope He has given. You have been made more than a conqueror. He has given you everything you need to walk in this mission. God has a great position for you. Therefore, have faith in the keeper of your soul.

Let Go

Are you hanging on to everything that has happened to you? Is the reason the pain of a separation, the rebelliousness of a child, the backstabbing of a friend, or the results of being alone? These things were not meant to be held on to. They were meant to help you understand yourself better. God wants you to know what you are able to do. Life will bring many problems, but they are to prepare you for what He has intended for you.

A separation may be very hurtful. It may make you look back and wonder why you invested so much time in something that was obviously not going to work. You begin to hold on to the regret, the guilt, and how foolish you feel for staying as long as you did. The problem is, you felt false security holding on to what could have been. Sometimes the old must be cut off to make room for the new. There is a greater blessing in store for those who trust God.

A rebellious child can make you hold on too many emotions, blaming yourself for the rebellion. However, the child's actions are just a trick of the devil to distract you from what is really going on. God may be using this situation to teach you how to pray and intercede. Oh yes, there will be hurts and pains, but bow before the One who knows all. He will lead you in this assignment.

Now, the hurt of friends and the betrayal by family members will always cut with an unbearable deepness. Nevertheless, you must love them even though they are killing you softly. The question is, can you forgive them for selling you into slavery and falsely accusing you, finally resulting in an emotional prison, which is what happened to Joseph? That may not be your exact experience, but their actions can cause similar situations. It may result in being a slave to emotional drama, untrue accusations, and finally being captive to the feeling of being forsaken.

Joseph had to endure each intricate component of his assignment to be placed in a position to help his family. Your family and friends my hurt you, but the love of God will lead you to their deliverance. This is only if you endure the necessary stages of your assignment, which will place you in a position to bring them out of their hardship.

As you know, loneliness has a way of bringing all things to light. It will reveal the need to be close to God, the need to intercede concerning your child, and the seriousness of being placed in a position to rescue your family. You have been chosen, and you must be familiar with the ingredients that go along with being God's choice. You must let go, because your situations will mold and make you into what God intended. The past, present, and future have all been predestined for you.

Release It

Let go of all the disappointments and even the pain.
Don't hold back the tears; let it rain.

Let go of the doubt that you can love again.
Embrace hope and know it will be who God sends.

There are no failures in this race
If you trust in God and keep the pace.

Striving to enter in at the straight gate,
Releasing love in place of hate.

Walking with a victorious stride,
Sins are forgiven; there's nothing to hide.

Standing strong in the Lord and in the power of His might,
You are now free to love; there's no longer a fight.

Breakers are gone and the pieces returned.
To gain your heart and love, it must be earned.

You are whole and also complete.
You are God's child. Let go and release.

It Still Hurts

You have decided in your mind; *I will let the sufferings of this test prepare me for my assignment.* You have placed all in the hands of God, regardless of how difficult it may seem. You have learned to let go. The outcome of your obedience is up to God. He knows the end from the beginning. Your life is a tale that has been told. You have decided to let the story God wrote before the foundations of the world play out fully, without your interference.

Although your decision is settled and you are prepared for what is to come, there are still hurts. There is still the pain of letting go, the pain of pruning. The pain of being alone is working for your good. Even though you understand why the storm has come, it doesn't ease any of the pain. Praying and staying in the presence of God is your only medication. This prescription is sure to help you face the pain and stand the test.

Your breakthrough is closer than you think, and you will appreciate everything that is necessary to arrive in the place where you will be. Just keep in mind, God knows just what it takes to get you to let go.

Especially Yours

There are many questions about who you will be when God is finished. Where will you be and what will you do? You are asking Him about yourself. You want to know why He chose you for this task. He has given you a new identity and adopted you into His family. He is protecting the investment He has made in you. Why does He love you so much?

But then you think, *When it is all said and done, Lord, You have the last word.* That word from God is, "I have greatness planned for you. I have a position that was designed for only you to hold. I have a work so divine that most would not believe it was designed for your hands and heart to operate.

"I am planning something so special for you, just because you want me. I love you and have chosen you, and want to bless you with a holy inheritance. All I require from you is obedience. Hold on to my hand and don't let go. I will take you higher than you have ever been, to places you have never seen. I will meet you in the garden in the coolness of the day and share my plans with you. You are my friend."

Easy to Love You

I am at peace when I stand with my man.
He places his life and his wife in God's hands.

I am at peace when I stand with my wife.
She gives God her man and dedicates her life.

With each embrace, I am safe; there's no fear.
We seek His presence and our union is so dear.

We are His flowers to hold,
His clay to mold,
and His spirits to control.

As one we will work for our God, our Creator.
I'm her husband, she's my wife, and I thank God that He made her.

This holy union let no man put asunder.
What holds us together is the power of God, and this power is a wonder.

Father, God, for our love we adore and all praises are due,
And our union will display the power You hold,
and how easy it is to love You.

Your Wait Is Ordained;
It Is Not in Vain

God has ordained certain things to take place in your life. These things will be manifested in an appointed time. Nothing you do or say can force, stimulate, or even cause them to happen any sooner. You have to be aware and realize that God has a predestined time for all things to occur and a time for you to receive what's predestined.

These things are intentional. The hand of God has fashioned everything so that it will work for your good. Make sure you trust the leading and direction of God for its fulfillment. You may think you can comprehend and understand the fullness, but God is in control. Therefore, it is much bigger than you can ever imagine. So, if God places it in your hands at this time, it would cease to exist entirely. God wants glory at a larger magnitude than you can produce.

However, He wants to bless you in the process. Your wait is not in vain; your wait is ordained. There is glory in your future. Wait on the Lord, and trust Him. It will not be long now. The struggle is almost over. You may say you cannot see a way in or a way out. But God is in control, so whether you see it or not, He opens the doors and leads. Just follow Him. He knows where to go and where you need to be.

It Is Almost Over

You may have gotten to a point where you are wondering, *Is it all worth it?* But now is the time you should hold on for dear life! You have reached the end. Some people get to within days, hours, or minutes from the release of their blessings and throw in the towel. When everything seems to be intensifying, and all hell has broken loose, demons have gotten new assignments and you feel them on your trail, it is only a sign that you are near the end.

This is a time of rejoicing because everything that can be thrown at you is being thrown. You are stepping out of the trial, the test, and the tribulation, and Satan does not want that. If he can make you fall at the finish line before crossing, you will have to start over. Do not give up. Do not fall. Run, run, run with the patience, the strength, and the endurance you acquired during the tests. It is time to put what you have learned to work.

You are not the same. This test has taken you to places you had never visited. You have seen God in a whole new light. He has developed you. Your destiny is before you. All your failures and disappointments are behind you. Hold your head up, because you have won this race. Prepare yourself for the next. You are more than a conqueror. Now ask yourself, *What is a conqueror?* A conqueror is one who defeats and captures. God has given you the city. Walk in your victory and authority. You win!

My Lord

Lord—a person who has authority, control, or power over others; a master, chief, or ruler

God—the one Supreme Being, the creator, and ruler of the universe

My first book, *The Fulfillment of Your Destiny*, describes something that I am personally experiencing. I am walking those pages daily. I am sure my readers can relate as they turn the pages of that book. I really was the first partaker of the fruits God produced through me on the pages as prophecies came to pass in my life. At this juncture in my life I realize I am entering the latter part of the first book ("True Destiny"). Clearly, I have learned that I will retrace the book over and over until perfection. I will do so until that great and perfect day when my Lord comes for me.

I have been instructed to release everything that I hold dear. Not to forsake it, but not to hold it too close to my heart. There is room for only one. He wants me to entirely trust and depend on Him. This task may sound like an easy endeavor to some. However, when you have lived a life in which you trusted what was at your grasp, you tend to find it difficult to let go of such dependencies.

My Lord will not accept pieces of my heart; He demands it all at this time. It is very important that I let Him have His way concerning my heart. I release all, that I may have Him. This journey is at its end, and the result depends on whether I followed all the instructions. Trust and dependence should be only in and on Him. If I am to come out victoriously, prepared for the next level, I must allow Him to be my Lord, not just my God. There is a great difference between Him being my God and Him being my Lord. On this journey, He will always be identified as my

Lord. But He will demonstrate His godly supremacy to all those who fight against me.

Reality Check

Have you considered that what you assumed to be the will of God is actually a reality you created? It did not start out that way. You followed the plan, and of course there were times when you failed, but you repented and continued in the faith. However, there was a tested situation with which you got a little too personal, too close, too attached. Now it is part of your created reality. You slowly drifted like a dry, broken log in the easy flow of a calm river. What you have failed to realize is that at the end of the river, there is a fall. Your creation will result in your failure.

Your assignment was there to teach you, to promote growth. Unfortunately, you embraced the assignment with other intentions. This is the time to check your reality; your conception of the objective was totally outside the will of God. The major problem is that you started to rely on your view and how you envisioned the thing to be.

Now your assignment has become an attachment. You must release this attachment and move in the perfect will of God. It is possible that this attachment was destined for another time and you birthed it prematurely. As a result, it will suffer from delays, weaknesses, dependencies, and everything else that is associated with a rash decision. Stick with the plan.

The worst thing you can do now is try to figure out the plan. You made a lot of progress through your obedience to the will of God. Release this attachment and return to the mission. God has planned a blessed life for you. What you choose is not nearly as great as what the divine planner has for you. Trust Him and He will shock your socks off. Things will fall into place when you allow God to lead. Sometimes God prevents you from things to protect you. These problems are not unlikely at all; they happen to Christians when they relax their standards and begin to feel overly confident.

Although you have overcome this very difficult trial, stay on guard; Satan is waiting for the perfect opportunity to trap you again. Yes, you are stronger now that you have endured, but there will be other trials, tests, and temptations, at an increased level. If you trust and believe in God for the outcome, you will be just fine. He has it all under control.

Learning to Forgive

On this journey, there are things you will have to let go of. Your destiny, your assignment, and your mission are now in progress. Nevertheless, through each stage of this process, there will be a period of letting go. Past hurts and disappointments will play a huge role in whether you are successful. You must complete each assignment in its appointed time. These physical and emotional pains are disappointments and failures that have become avenues of misaligned development. Holding on to these things will only build their strength over you.

God's plan for you will involve you walking in complete freedom. He wants your testimony to be free of contamination. Each trial you encounter during this walk will build character, relationships, and a greater desire to please God. But if you have a small amount of unforgiveness in your heart, God will not allow you to move forward. If you desire a full and complete understanding of God's will for your life, then you must rid yourself of the hindrances. Examine yourself to identify the hindrances. Have confidence that God has your best interests at heart.

You Can Make Mistakes;
Don't Let Mistakes Make You

As you continue to walk in this divine call, you will encounter mistakes and endure some failures. They will affect you, but your mission and your assignment was predestined and made just for you. Your awareness of this information should also reveal that these mistakes do not have the power to make you.

If you are not careful, you will find yourself being re-created by situations and shortcomings. It was not intended for circumstances to turn you away from God. Their effect should only cause you to seek God even more, to call on His name, and of course to trust Him. Your situations and circumstances should have the ability to develop fully what God has put in you.

You are complete in Christ; each of your experiences should initiate growth. For example, consider a budding flower. In its beginnings, it is complete, although you cannot see its potential: a seed originally requiring nothing. It has everything necessary to be a mature flower, even in its beginning stages. The ingredients held within will be developed and matured through the process of development. When it sprouts, a seed must go through the hardness of the ground before you can see its design. Therefore, know that what is in you will be developed through your trials and tribulations. Mistakes are part of development. Remember, you cannot be made if you have already been created.

All Good and Perfect Gifts Come from God

Okay, you are in the middle of your assignment. You are not struggling as much as you thought you would, but it is still not the easiest thing you have done. There appears to be a blessing in the middle of your assignment, but you are a little unsure about it.

You are praying, fasting, and seeking God for clarity. Your answer has already been given through the word of God. "Every good gift and every perfect gift is from above. And cometh down from the Father of lights, with whom is no variableness, neither shadow of turning" (James 1:17, KJV). Now, look at this blessing and hold it up to the word of God. Is the gift good? That's only one component. Is the gift perfect? That's the second component. This is how you will be made aware that the gift is of God. You may say nothing is perfect. Go again to the word of God to identify what He considers perfect for you. In Genesis 6:9, 2 Samuel 22:33, and
1 Chronicles, it is God who makes the thing perfect.

Therefore, is God involved in the blessing? Gifts are blessings from the Lord. If the blessing is not of sin but of righteousness, then it is a blessing given by the Father of lights. When you begin to realize that you are in the stream that flows with the blessings of God, then and only then will you open your heart and receive an overflow.

(Gift of God)

"Every man also to whom God hath given riches and wealth, and hath given him power to eat thereof, and to take his portion, and to rejoice in his labor; this is the gift of God" (Ecclesiastes 5:19, KJV).

(Gift of God)

"Jesus answered and said unto her, if thou knewest the gift of God, and who it is that saith to thee, give me to drink; thou wouldest have asked of him, and he would have given thee living water" (John 4:10, KJV).

(Gift of God)

"For I, would that all men were even as I myself. But every man hath his proper gift of God, one after this manner, and another after that" (1 Corinthians 7:7, KJV).

(Gift of God)

"Wherefore I put thee in remembrance that thou stir up the gift of God, which is in thee by the putting on of my hands" (2 Timothy 1:6, KJV).

Once you have grasped the concept that exposes the gifts of God, you will be free to give and receive the gift that is within you.

Now Take His Head

You have stood against the giant. You chose your weapon and have taken him down. You have proclaimed to this uncircumcised Philistine that the Lord Almighty is your God and that this day the Philistine will be destroyed. However, many Saints have made the same proclamation and have also chosen their weapon, which indeed knocked out their giant.

Unfortunately, there is something they have failed to do: they have failed to finish the job. You must take off the head of the giant (the situation, circumstances, family, job, or even your mind). The head represents power and authority. Therefore, if it stays intact, the giant will still rule over you. You see, you knocked him out, but you did not destroy him. He will recover.

You must remove the control, the power, and the authority with the sword, which is the word of God. You can knock the giant out with the weapon with which God has equipped you. However, you must realize that it is going to take obedience combined with the power of God to take the head off this thing. You have been given the power, the control, and the authority from the Creator of the universe, who has made His dwelling place in you.

Although at this point you have gained control over your giant, I must remind you that fear can cause you to lose that control. But if you go before the thing with confidence in God, He will deliver you from all forms of captivity. Your battle weapons and armor will not be of this world. The weapons of your warfare are not carnal but are mighty through God to the pulling down of strongholds.

What you will use for this victory will be the familiar, the thing that has been tested in the fire. It is what God has equipped you with for the completion of your destiny. You are equipped and secured with everything you need to overcome your giants.

My Song in the Night

Life has many twists and turns, and it may appear that you are faced with a new challenge at every turn. This should not be a surprise to you, because challenges come with the territory. Even with this knowledge, you continue trying to figure out which way to turn in hopes of avoiding another challenge. At this point things are overwhelming and hard to bear, but in the midst of this darkness, remember, the battle is indeed the Lord's, and He will present you as a victorious warrior. However, you will have times that are not favorable.

In your journey there will be times when you will appreciate every struggle, every trial, and every challenge because of where it has brought you from and where it will carry you. These trials and struggles are your night experiences; they represent times of darkness in your life. But God is your song in the night. He is the song that causes the chains to fall off and the prison doors to open. Your song in the night will save you from what was intended to take your life. Your song is a song of deliverance. He is your song in the night. When your night approaches and the darkness comes, let your heart song overcome the darkness.

Breathe on Me

Lord, I want to sense Your presence near,
to know and have confidence that You are always here.

To feel Your anointing as it covers me,
To be surrounded by Your essence as far as my spirit can see.

To taste of Your word and let Your spirit abide,
My protector—within Your wing I will hide.

To drink from that well that never runs dry,
To soar in my spirit with my Lord on high.

To smell Your fragrance on my body and in my soul,
It is that very fragrance that has made my life whole.

To be so close that Your breath I can feel,
To stay there until all my wounds are healed.

To release my care as Your arms surround me entirely
And rest in Your grace as Your spirit breathes on me.

He Is in the Midst

You desire a greater move, you seek to hear a word, and you wait on the promises. All that you wait for is present as you gather with the saints. The things you seek from the Lord can be found when you fail not to assemble yourself with the believers. God is in the midst, and He has everything you desire and require for the success of the mission He has assigned to you. When you are in agreement with Saints on the things, God will show up.

He wants to answer your request, and He also wants to meet with you. "Come now, and let us reason together, saith the Lord: though your sins be as scarlet, they shall be as white as snow; though they be red like crimson, they shall be as wool" (Isaiah 1:18, KJV).

If there are things you need to be before the Lord to receive clarity, He is there to give it. He won't leave you in confusion. You have to pass in His presence if you want Him to move. One very important thing that you must remember is that you need the saints.

Don't isolate yourself. That is a trick of the enemy. Don't lose the blessing, the gift that is found in the midst. If you want to meet with the Father, then get with His children. Call on your Daddy in agreement, He is a faithful father. What He says, He will perform. If you follow in complete obedience, He will be there in the midst. He will not only show up, but bring a blessing. He is your Father, and He will never leave you hopeless or helpless.

My Refuge

The Lord is your help; see Him in your present storm. Your associations did not cause this storm. It is an appointed storm at an appointed time. This storm was designed especially for you. At times in your life, you will face winds that seem to blow your mind. If you are secure and have the mind of Christ, no storm can take you out of position. There will be floods in your life that will seem to rise above your head, but no waters will be able to overtake you. The floods of the living waters are the only waters able to take you.

There will be rains that never seem to cease, but the rains will stop, the winds will cease, and the flood will subside. And this is the result of your obedience in the storm. God will be your hiding place. When it is overwhelming, you can run to the Lord for help. He is your peace in the middle of the storm. He is your way of escape. God will allow storms, but He will also provide a safe place in Him. Do not fear, because He has a promise for you. He is leading you in the way that you should go. He will stand in your defense and cover you.

Your Wounds Are Still Tender

You were under the impression that you were over those hurts, those disappointments, those failures, and those rejections. The only way you will know that you are completely over those wounds is to successfully handle similar issues without allowing the old wounds to interfere. If those wounds are still tender, they will begin to run and burn when you encounter similar situations—running with self-doubt, lack of understanding, unforgiveness, and other emotions that were involved with the previous hurts.

When those tender places are tampered with, you will react in a way that is not pleasing to God or beneficial to your spiritual maturity. There must be a time to allow the wounds to heal. They cannot heal while being held open by identical situations. Hurting people will hurt others. Sometimes it will be intentional, and other times it will be unintentional.

However, at the first sign that you have suffered hurt, give yourself time to heal. When there are hurts, unfortunately, others will be affected by your hurting environment. The divine mission God has for you will ensure healing if you allow it. He needs a healed and whole person to administer the healing medication to others. And this medication is your life. You must allow a period of time or season of restoration. God has everything in His control. Let Him heal you from whatever you are dealing with or whatever left the wounds.

There is nothing too hard for our God. He finds pleasure in mending your brokenness. If you will rely on the Lord completely, you will know when it is time to move on. Your success depends on your obedience to the words and direction of God. Do not take the easy road; take the road that God assigned to you. This is the path that He has made plain. This is the one that has a light for your feet. You will clearly see the direction in which you must go.

You Were in Him

In the beginning, God created the heavens and the earth. But where were you? You say you hadn't been created yet. I agree that your body was not yet created. However, you did exist. You were with Him. You ask, *How could that be?* When the firmaments were established, you were with Him. When the land, the sea, the vegetation, and even the stars, moon, and sun were created, you were with Him. And on the sixth day, the precious vessel that would contain you was created with His love and care.

The body was fashioned, and every detail was completed. He breathed not on, but inside, the vessel and watched it come alive. You became a living soul, the greatest of all creations. He brought life outside of Himself and created individual lives. Nobody but God can do such a great thing.

"According, as He has chosen us in him before the foundations of the world, that we should be holy and without blame before him in love" (Ephesians 1:4, KJV).

In the Hands of God

God will keep you through all you have to face in the fulfilling of your destiny. If you trust His leading, you will always find yourself in His perfect will. He wants you to trust Him with your heart, because in all reality, it is the heart that decides (Deuteronomy 11:13). God wants your heart in His hand, for that is the part of you that is passionate, emotional, and will commit. If you will surrender your heart to Him, He will never break it. He will only add more love, compassion, and peace to it. He wants you to rest in His hands and be confident that you are protected.

Once you are in the hands of God, no one can remove you. Only you will have the power to change your position. The love that the Father has for you is unlike that of a natural man. He does not get irritated with you wanting to spend time with Him. Actually, the more time you spend with Him, the more you will take on His characteristics. He desires you to be more like Him. The way you praise, pray, fast, and even meditate creates the glory He desires.

In His hands, you will find answers. In His hands, you will be made whole. In His hands is where you will see Him demonstrate and manifest Himself for your sake. Staying in the hands of God will be no secret. Those around you will observe that being in His hands improves your position in life. These spectators will see your life and crave the same, and as a result, they would reap the benefits of their imitation. There is joy in knowing that you are safe and complete in His hands. He is operating on your behalf concerning the unseen and unknown things. He is preparing you as the potter prepares the clay.

He makes you a vessel of honor because you are His and you are devoted to Him. You are in love with Him and persuaded that nothing will separate you from His love. You have come to the conclusion that out of His hands you are lost and wandering in the wilderness without guidance. The reality is that you need God to go before you and surround you. You are covered by God's hands.

Don't Retaliate; Let God Fight

There will be hurts and disappointments as you walk in your call. And many times, those close to you are the cause of these situations. But do not retaliate. You must forgive. If you fight, you will lose. You will be fighting the wrong thing. You must realize that the people are not the problem.

If you resort to retaliation, your will make yourself the problem. Search and examine yourself and determine the problems that are preventing your spiritual success. Of course, you know Satan is trying everything in his power to cause your demise. Nevertheless, God is there to give you your life and give it to you more abundantly.

No matter how it looks, God doesn't plan defeat, only victory. He will cause great confusion to all who come against you. No weapon formed against you will prosper. You are more than a conqueror. Because of who Christ has become in you, you are an overcomer. Let them talk, let them throw stones, and let them forsake you. Your relationship with God is the most important relationship you should have. This communion with God is able to keep you in all things. But other relationships can and will possibly fall.

Choose your battle carefully. Evaluate the necessity of fighting. Is it worth fighting for? What is the gain? You should never fight in vain. If someone speaks falsely against you and you retaliate with hurtful words, ask yourself what the profit was. Did it bring glory to God? Were you edified? If there is no gain, glory, or edification, then leave that battle in the hands of God.

He will bring you victory. He will condemn the tongue that rises against you. He will be a refuge in the time of the storm. Hide in Him. When Sanballat and Tobiah came against Nehemiah, he prayed to God.

"Hear us, O our God, for we are despised. Turn their insults back on their own heads. Give them over as plunder in a land of captivity. Do not cover up their guilt or blot out their sins from your sight, for they have thrown insults in the face of the builders" (Nehemiah 4:4–5, KJV).

He knew that God could do more that he could to repay them for what they did against His people. Trust God, and the outcome will produce deliverance. God will work it out for you. He will use what the devil meant for your destruction and create greatness in you.

Battle Scars

If you refuse to allow the Lord to fight for you, it will result in unnecessary battle scars. Because of your decision to fight and retaliate, you will suffer at the hands of your enemy. Your decision has left you exposed. God cannot be responsible for what you encounter at this point. You have made the choice to place matters in your own hands.

Therefore, your stepping out has resulted in battle scars, which have left you exposed. The decision you made caused your removal from the covering. Now you are subjected to harm. You will acquire scars because of this position. Your decision to retaliate may be associated with trying to clear your name, because of false allegations. It may be a situation about finances or family issues. Nevertheless, you must not assume the position as the one with the answers, because you have none. Allow the Lord to handle every opposing situation. He can get quicker and better results when you allow Him to fight for you.

Deal with It Now

There are so many things that you have put off. You've put them off because you have concluded that they have nothing to do with your walk with God. Everything that you encounter in your life must be dealt with. It cannot be left alone in the hope that it will disappear. Do not continue to put it off or cover it up, because it will take ground and begin to grow and produce. Sooner or later it will get to the point of overgrown, choking weeds.

It may have seemed small and insignificant, but when left in the fertile ground of unforgiveness, jealousy, or strife, it will become a bigger problem than before. Deal with all situations in their infancy stages. Do not give them time to grow. The Lord will instruct you concerning the removal of potential problems. Nothing should be left to grow when it has the potential to be damaging. Complete removal is absolutely necessary. The more aware you become in the things of the Lord, the more you will know and understand how to handle and deal with it now.

Life has a price.

What are you willing to pay?

Now, what's your value?

—January 28, 2008
Angela Lee-Easter

Something Better Is Coming

Do not settle for the here and now. Do not settle, because God has planned more for your life. If you decide that you are content with your present position and refuse to move because of familiarity, then you have caused the move of God to cease concerning your life. God has planned more for you and desires to release more to you. However, you must accept the move and position yourself to receive it.

He will multiply every area of your life if you are ready. Let Him bless you as He desires. Do not hinder your blessings. Do not hinder your growth. Do not hinder the blessing that will come through you to others. There has been too much invested in you concerning the kingdom; therefore He requires your submission, obedience, and humbleness to manifest His investment. You carry a valuable gift, and this gift has the ability to break and destroy yokes. It has the ability to create change in the atmosphere and in the environment.

The changes that can be stimulated through your gift can cause a mind to change from doubt to faith. Your gift is unique. That is why it is important that you submit to the move of God. As you walk in your gift, you will experience the direct power of God in your call. You will not be just a spectator of this power; it will be on you, in you, and working through you. This is the will of God. Something better is coming. It can come only if you release the old and step into the new. Those better things rely on you. Remember, you are a vessel to be used by God. He created, fashioned, and molded you in a particular way for a particular purpose. You may not understand it all now, but trust Him to manifest His perfect will in you.

Made for Me

He is like no other, a man of integrity.
He is the man that God has made for me.

He is strong in the word and trusts God completely.
He is the man that God has made for me.

He is running this race, and at the end you will see
He is the man that God has made for me.

Just as God sent His Son to die
and set me free,
He also sent this man that He has made for me.

Finding me, lost in God's eternity,
He is the man that God has made for me.

Now, I am found in his arms, where I want to be.
I am with the man God has made for me.

Where Is the Line Located?

Now that you are in position, you must be careful of the deception of the enemy. He wants you to play and deal with the old things. He will instantly tell you it is okay. He tries to persuade you to get close to the things of the world. His plan is to get you out into the deep, with no escape. If you are aware of his tricks and deception, you will never cross the line. You are in a great position, walking in obedience to the will of God.

Are you wondering how close you can get to the line without sinning? If you can see the line from where you are positioned, you are too close. In God's arms, the line is a distant thought. In God's arms, the line has nothing to offer. The line is where Satan hides out, seeking those he can devour. He is at the line with the guarantee of failure, defeat, and sin, but God guarantees victory.

Now that you have successfully walked in the will of God, you must avoid ever crossing the line, because Satan will attempt to kill you while on the other side. You are a threat to his kingdom because of what God has placed within you. There is greatness in you. You are a constant reminder that he was once great. But remember, no weapon formed against you will prosper. Shake yourself and keep on moving. If you resist the devil, he will flee, if you draw near to God, He will draw near to you. It is up to you. The line is not the problem, because it has been established. To get near the line, you have to move in its direction. It is a decision you must make. It is not the line that will cause problems; it is you. The safest place in the whole wide world is in the will of God, and that place is nowhere near the line.

What Is the Next Step?

"He sees everything I do, and every step I take" (Job 31:4–6, TLB).

"Direct my footsteps according to thy words: let no sin rule over me" (Psalm 119:133, KJV).

"In his heart a man plans his course, but the Lord determines his steps" (Proverbs 16:9, ESV).

Every step in this decision you make must be ordered by God. At no time should you assume or try to guess what you are to do. Your destiny relies on your obedience to instruction. Do not make a move without it being confirmed by God. You see, your obedience to His will affects you and all those God has assigned to you. It would be selfish and irresponsible to move on your own assumptions. You are to bless the kingdom. So, think about your vows to God. He is expecting you to keep your word.

No matter the mistakes, failures, or disappointments, He expects you to do and be what you vowed. Your promised commitment is absolutely necessary. God must order your next step. Where you are at this very moment must be validated. God must let you know that where you are, is where you should be. Make sure you wait until you receive that confirmation. Because if you are standing in the wrong place, then every step from this point will be wrong. Moving is not the first thing of importance; hearing God and obeying is first and foremost.

God Is Good

Psalm 118:1

God is good. God is good—amen. Why is He good? This is a statement that we hear almost every day. God is good. You must place in your mind why He is good. Not because of what He has done in another, but because of what He has done in you personally. God is good to me: at age nineteen, I sat for many days and thought about taking my life, but He gave me hope. God is good: at age twenty-three, I was told in the emergency room that if I had not come that night, I would have died of a heart attack. For ten years, I carried a sickness that consumed my life. I was the lady with the issue of blood.

However, I continued to work full time, raising a small child, and enrolled in college full time. I kept my life as normal as it could possibly be. I was told in my twenties that I couldn't have more children. Today, I am alive and completely whole with a miracle child, two-year-old Joydan. God is good. Now, what you must do is place in your mind what He has done for you. Then when you say God is good, it will not be just a filler in a service or conversation; it will be a testimony of where He has brought you from.

Do You Remember?

Remember when you were in Egypt and He brought you across the Red Sea? Remember when He carried you through the wilderness, feeding and dressing you, and finally releasing you to the Land of Promise? Do not forget that once you arrived in Canaan, you abandoned God. Remember, He did not destroy you but allowed you to be carried away to a strange land of captivity. Remember the day you became as dry bones and God's love sent you a word through the wind? He spoke, and you became a mighty army. Remember: although you fail, He will never leave you or forsake you.

Begin to reminisce about the things you know that God has done for you. Reminisce about how He brought you out and gave you a land flowing with milk and honey. Because of His faithfulness, your needs are met. He is a God that keeps His promises. Your hopes are attended to and fulfilled because He loves you.

From this point on, when you hear or say that God is good, place a memory in your head of something He has done for you—something no one else can perform. Remember that His grace and mercy delivered you in the midst of your created storm and then praise Him for His undying love.

Who Is This Man?

I was lost and He discovered me.
I was blind, but with His light, I now clearly see.
I was broken and full of doubt.
He mended my pieces and brought me out.

Who is this man that stands before me?
Who is this man that restored my sanity?
Who is this man that gave me a life so complete?
And in his fight for me, I gained the victory.

I lie in his bosom and now I am resting.
He is the man that gave me salvation's blessings.

No longer do I seek to be discovered
For He has found me,
And He is my true lover.

Know Your Judas

There will always be a Judas around. Judases are designed with a purpose, and that purpose is to help you get closer to fulfilling your God-given destiny. God has the power and the authority to choose how He uses the vessels He has created. He can use His vessels to hold things of value or to be discarded. If you are used and refused, your true worth has been revealed. Judas had purpose, and because of his choices, he was discarded.

The Judas in your life will betray you, deceive you, and attempt to steal from you. Judas is all about advancement for himself, regardless of who may be hurt in the process. You are just a means to an end, and that end is to satisfy the lust within. These are a few characteristics of Judas. Nevertheless, your response to your Judas must mirror Christ's response to His.

Once you recognize your Judas and his purpose in your life, do not reject him, but embrace him. He has been placed in your life with a greater purpose. You must understand that destiny requires many types of people for its fulfillment. Situations you encounter that produce struggles or misfortunes are often connected with your Judas.

Your Judas will stay close to you. He will know your likes and dislikes. If you did not know any better, you would consider this person a friend. In any case, take this advice: never let this person close to your heart. If you allow him or her in, your heart may become pierced, stabbings may occur, and you will become victim to carrying a load for someone else. Those are the results of loving such a one.

You have to understand that although you don't need to carry the sins of your past, Judas will remind you of your sins, weaknesses, and condition. What you must appreciate is that Judas is just a vehicle to mobilize you in the direction of your destiny. It is not Judas's desire to help you succeed. His desire is to gain, increase, or be promoted. Thinking about whether he hurt or damaged you will result in making his ambitions possible. What he intended for bad, God used for good?

If you trust God for the outcome, you will always come out on top. It does not matter what the intentions were for your demise. Your success is predetermined. God had you in mind a long time ago. Therefore, your life, once surrendered to Christ, is secure. God has a plan for you just as He had a plan for Judas. If you give yourself to Him, He will use you for His glory. If you give yourself to Satan, then you will be a pun in Satan's hands. You will be moving according to his every whim.

Just remember, God has Satan on a leash. He is Satan's boss man. So, God will allow Satan to use your Judas to push you to the path that leads you to fulfill your destiny. Judas may bring chaos, but this chaos is just a natural storm that will destroy the things that are not rooted, making room for new things to grow. Do not deny your Judas. Allow him the kiss of betrayal and move on in your destiny. When it is finished, you will be in a place to bless the kingdom. If you bring God glory through obedience, you will receive a greater weight of glory once you have endured your trial. God has a plan for you; now trust Him for the outcome.

Take the City

As a worshipper, you possess the power to take the city. That city can represent anything in your life that has fortified walls of pain, hurt, and disappointments. As a matter of fact, God has said that you are more than conquerors. But you must follow His instructions. Those instructions say that you must worship if you are going to take the city or possess the land.

The walls of Jericho fell during praise, but first they obeyed God's word. His words are received during your time of worship and adoration toward Him. Your blessings are in your obedience. You want to conquer the city. You want to get out of the hellish situation you are in and create an environment that is conducive to you having an abundant life. If this is what you seek, then you must allow your life to become a sacrifice that is holy and acceptable to the Lord.

Your decision to deny what you desire and what you have prayed for in order to worship makes your sacrifice sufficient unto God. This decision has the power to take others to take the city with you. You are not able to take the city alone. Special groups will accompany you. These groups will have the ability to follow God's plan without questioning it. His plan will develop you into a conqueror and an overtaker. You will take and possess the thing you seek to have. At the same time, you will obtain all that the city possessed. If you are willing and obedient, God will make you able to do what no one thought was possible. God will be there doing the work; you will just be there reaping the benefits as a true worshipper.

Not Everything Will Be a Struggle

Not everything you receive from the Lord will require struggle. Many Christians are under the impression that to acquire any good thing from the Lord, they have to fight, struggle, or go through tremendous difficulties. This is far from being the truth. Of course, some things will necessitate great effort on your part, but that is not to push you backward. Its true purpose is to open your eyes to what you will be and how you will fulfill your call. You are responsible for many of the things you are facing. The greater the request, the greater the test. Tests and trials are not to discourage you; they are allowed to strengthen and prepare you.

God knows all about the treasure you possess in your earthen vessel. Unfortunately, you are not very aware of the power of the treasure. Therefore, the things you encounter are to reveal your strength and power to possess what is already yours. When you trust God in all things, He positions you exactly where you need to be. This place will allow you to obtain the promise. In this journey, remember that it is your duty to give God what He desires: your praise. And as you give Him what truly belongs to Him, He will hold all the pieces together. True praise comes from a heart that is whole and filled with the love of God.

*Your heart belongs to the Lord.
It is to be whole and complete in His loving
arms, never to be broken or in pieces again.*

About the Author

Angela Lee-Easter, MEd, MCM, BBA

Angela was born and raised in a small town located in North Carolina. She learned at an early age the importance of knowing and talking to the Lord. Her mother, a single parent, taught Angela and her siblings to acknowledge God in all things. As Angela grew older, she realized that knowing about God and having a relationship of communion with Him were two very different things.

On November 28, 1990, seven days after her twentieth birthday, she committed her life to the Lord. She soon learned that this new life was not as easy as she had imagined it would be. She began to grow in the understanding of God's power to keep her. Although God never changed, she found herself fighting and struggling with her past, because of hurtful encounters she had been too young to control and later choices that caused physical, mental, and emotional damage.

These situations caused pieces of her life to be out of place. As the years passed, she began to realize that the only way to regain order in her life was to reclaim the pieces. To be whole once again depended on her success in this matter. When her life was aligned with the word of God, she was able to identify the broken pieces and experience God's promises in abundance. This choice gave her a new lease on life. The life she desired was the life God gave. To be made whole is to give God contr

www.ingramcontent.com/pod-product-compliance
Lightning Source LLC
Chambersburg PA
CBHW081017040426
42444CB00014B/3244